Pebble® Plus

Cats, Cats, Cats

Cat Behavior

by Christina Mia Gardeski

CAPSTONE PRESS
a capstone imprint

Pebble Plus is published by Capstone Press,
1710 Roe Crest Drive, North Mankato, Minnesota 56003
www.mycapstone.com

Library of Congress Cataloging-in-Publication Data
Cataloging-in-publication information is on file with the Library of Congress.
ISBN 978-1-5157-0956-5 (library binding)
ISBN 978-1-5157-1122-3 (ebook PDF)

Editorial Credits
Jaclyn Jaycox, editor; Philippa Jenkins, designer;
Pam Mitsakos, media researcher; Steve Walker, production specialist

Photo Credits
Alamy: Juniors Bildarchiv GmbH, 9; Getty Images: Hill Street Studio, 19; Shutterstock: Diana Taliun, 21, Dmitri
Ma, 7, Grey Carnation, 13, kmsh, 1, 17, Koldunov Alexey, cover, Oksana Kuzmina, 3, back cover, red rose,
design element throughout, S. Castelli, 5, Sunny_baby, 11, The Len, 15

Note to Parents and Teachers

The Cats, Cats, Cats set supports national science standards related to life
science. This book describes and illustrates cat behavior. The images support
early readers in understanding the text. The repetition of words and phrases
helps early readers learn new words. This book also introduces early readers to
subject-specific vocabulary words, which are defined in the Glossary section.
Early readers may need assistance to read some words and to use the Table
of Contents, Glossary, Read More, Internet Sites, Critical Thinking Using the
Common Core, and Index sections of the book.

Printed and bound in China
PO007732LEOF16

Table of Contents

Why Do Cats Do That?

Cats hide in boxes and rub against your legs. Have you ever wondered why they do these things and more? Let's find out!

A Cat's Meow

Kittens meow to tell their mothers they are hungry or scared. But grown cats meow to tell people what they want. Most grown cats do not meow at other cats.

Marked By a Cat

Cats rub their bodies on people. This feels like a snuggle, but it is a mark. Cats leave their scent on the person. This tells other cats that person is their owner.

Kitty Kisses

Your cat stares at you with its eyes half open. Then it blinks slowly. Blink back! Some people think this is a cat's way of giving you a kiss.

Kneading Paws

Your cat starts to knead your lap.

It pushes its paws up and down.

Kittens do this to get milk from their

mother's belly. Grown cats often

knead when they are happy.

Telling Tails

Watch a cat's tail to see how the cat feels. Happy cats hold their tails high. The tail fur is flat. A cat that flicks its tail back and forth quickly is upset. Step back!

Cat-in-a-Box

Cats like to fit themselves into shoe boxes, suitcases, and other small spaces. They then watch what is happening around them. Small spaces make cats feel safe.

A Cat's Purr

Most cats purr when they are happy.
But some cats purr when they are
sick, hurt, or afraid. Newborn kittens
cannot see or hear. Their mother
purrs so they can find her.

On the Hunt

Today most pet cats don't need to hunt for food. But they still pretend to hunt. They might hunt and follow a person's feet. Then they pounce on them!

Glossary

flick—to make a quick movement

knead—to push up and down with the paws

meow—the call or cry made by a cat

newborn—just having been born

pounce—to jump on something suddenly and grab it

purr—to make a low soft sound; animals such as cats purr

scent—the smell of a person or thing

Read More

MacLachlan, Patricia, and Emily MacLachlan Charest. *Cat Talk*. New York: Katherine Tegen Books, 2013.

Murray, Julie. *Cats*. Family Pets. Minneapolis: Abdo Kids, 2015.

Olson, Gillia. *Pet Cats Up Close.* Pets Up Close. North Mankato, Minn.: Capstone Press, 2015.

Internet Sites

FactHound offers a safe, fun way to find Internet sites related to this book. All of the sites on FactHound have been researched by our staff.

Here's all you do:

Visit *www.facthound.com*

Type in this code: 9781515709565

Super-cool stuff!

Check out projects, games and lots more at
www.capstonekids.com

23

Critical Thinking Using the Common Core

- Cats knead by pushing their paws up and down. Why do they knead? (Key Ideas and Details)

- What does it mean when a cat is flicking its tail back and forth quickly? (Key Ideas and Details)

- Cats purr for many different reasons. What is purring? (Craft and Structure)

Index